Unveiled, Exhaled

Kyla Benford

BookLeaf Publishing

Presentation by *BookLeaf Publishing*

Web: www.bookleafpub.com

E-mail: info@bookleafpub.com

ISBN: 9789357441421

First edition 2023

This book is dedicated to the human race-every being wanting to find their place, journeying to attain freedom or simply desiring to just "be" in the midst of their life journey.

ACKNOWLEDGEMENT

I give all glory and praise to The Most High. Without His love, grace and mercy, neither I, nor this work of expression would be.

PREFACE

"Unveiled, Exhaled" is the byproduct of various emotions, thoughts and perspectives that I experienced while beginning to discover my likeness to The Most High, processing day-to-day living and learning to express myself more vividly. Some of the poems were cultivated over a span of 1-2 years ago and some were written during the actual composition of this book, as I tapped into past emotions even though the moments that they stemmed from are long gone. Each body of expression is rooted in the progressive decision of going inward, facing my fears and choosing to express myself from the core of my being-a universal road that I believe we are all meant to travel on.

Surrender

Tears cascade like waterfalls
And cleanse the surface
Of my cheeks

Conflictions climb to the surface
To finally be perceived

I'm then humbled,
Collapsing to my knees

My flesh proceeds to plead
But my soul
No longer wants to bleed

Can't go on with the greed
That disagrees
For my endlessness to succeed

It's either Him or it's me
I can't choose one
Only partly

I guess this is surrender,
A bittersweet apple tree.

Brand New

Being sensitive to ugly things
Means that you're aware
Of the beautiful ones too

Stimulated in a new dimension,
But the feeling is familiar

I'm vaguely convinced
That it isn't new

If I tried to change
The tender parts of me,
I'd no longer be free

I'm called and led
To live authentically

Trailblazing ain't always pretty
When branches and dirt
Diminish the view

Traveling into the unknown,
A place called "Brand New".

Done With Hiding

Tired of hiding
All that I'm meant to be

Arise and take flight
Like a newly matured eagle
From a long lived oak tree

Resorted to hiding
In order to survive

But the time has come
To thrive and dive
Into the abyss of destiny-

A mystery, yet sure
To evoke ecstasy

Bliss is birthed
By living in purpose-
And by sharing
Your unique humane service

With the inhabitants
Of this storefront
That houses you and I

Done with hiding
In order to survive

A new me is knocking,
Ready to live alive

A new me is equipped,
Aware that sacred assistance
Is on my side

A new me is unapologetic
And taking her time.

Be Still & Know

I took a step back
To finally feel the wind
Enter into my nostrils again

I succumbed
To the yearning
To intentionally be still-

A rebellion against society,
A revolt against the culture
That breeds destination anxiety

How deficient is this life
If not in tune with my Creator?

If I'm rushing to be
Where He never sent me,
With a heart full of idolatry,
Am I really becoming greater?

Am I fulfilling my mission
If I’m crammed
With carnal minded cognition?

If I’m not Holy Spirit led,
How valuable are my intentions?

Be still and listen
It's time to pay attention.

Vegetation Adorned

What is it
About nature
That captivates the soul?

Could it be
That the atmosphere
Summons remembrance

Of God's original order
As the Holy Book has told?

What is it
About nature
That rejuvenates the soul?

Maybe it's the serenity;
In the whispers
Of the wind

Or in the washing
Of the waves

That whispers possibilities
Of God-dreams to unfold

To abide in nature
Is to dwell
In the presence of God.

He's everywhere,
All of the time

But if you need further evidence,
Gaze around you,
Seek Him,
And you'll find

Without Him,
Nothing in existence
Would be

So when I yield among greenery,
I'm not assigning
Sovereignty to the trees,
But to the Divinity,
Who grounds their foundation

And Who generates their emergence;
The King of all Kings.

Treasure Chest of Rest

Been through the fire
Maneuvered through the waters

Been met with angst
Found out I'm His daughter

Marked with grace
Now, I'm working smarter,
Not harder

No burnout on my plate,
No imposter syndrome as a starter

Rest is my treasure chest,
It's my beloved gold

In a society
That falsely molds
Sabbath as a futile venture

I recline with a smize
Painting my eyes

And with gratitude
Dripping from my skin,

Overflowing from within

After knowing
That I've done
All that I can do

My countenance reads
That I'm at ease

No need
To be displeased

When I've already submitted,
To My First Love,
All that I need.

Resilience

Shifting timelines,
Eradicating faulty guidelines

Living in the natural,
While enjoying
Supernatural amenities

Healing
Via heavenly remedies

You have this
Angelic-like energy
That is God-Grown,
God-sewn

The power
That you hold
Is a durable mold.

Deliverance

I go through deliverance
Every time I dive
Into the sacred waters
Of The Holy Bible

My consciousness
Is continuously renewed,
Transformed, enthused

All that is apprised
In Scripture
Is a life-jacket
Composed of miraculous Truths

I'm made a new creation
When Divine inspiration

Breaks the chains
And cuts the noose
From around my mind

And in due time,
My flesh, too,
Falls in line.

Wisdom

"Wisdom" is her name

She's groundbreaking
And crucial
To the game

In this bittersweet,
Riveting experience
That we call life

She opened up my soul-
My mind to be precise

My prediction?
She's transporting me
To higher heights

Excellence is detected
In my foreseeable future
All things of the Most High God

She speaks Truths
So unmovable
My spirit can't help but to nod

I'm in agreement and awe
Her knowing is remarkably raw

She shares counsel gifted
As generational inheritance

So that my children's children
No longer have to brawl

No generational wounds to confine
No depression to steal life's smiles
No anxiety to paralyze
No survival mode meant to immobilize

Freedom is our birthright.

Agape

I have undeniably experienced true love
And this transcendental mercy is affirmed
Every morning that I awaken

8,811 days later
And I'm still here.

I will rejoice in the day
That the Lord has made

When daybreak merges
With my soul's electrified urges

In each of those moments,
I've been graced
With the golden opportunity

To live seeing through my temple's rare lens,
Filtered by my God's Perfect Ways

Born again
After being
Torn again

That is how I know

That I am loved-
Supernaturally,
Miraculously,
Unconditionally

There's nothing I could have done
To deserve this.

Eternity

Since a child,
Eternity has been
In my heart.

Imagine my surprise
Once I realized

Eternity has been
God's plan all along.

Great Captain

Immense sadness
Comes in waves

I couldn't have predicted
This sudden change

But I know that
What's best for me

Isn't always initially
What I thought it'd be

How do I stay afloat?
Raging currents
Attempt to rule this boat

But I know a Great Captain

Who steers me
To serene scenes
Of cobalt satin

My wings
Caught an unforeseen blow
That knocked me off my pivot

Didn't want to lose it all
But my circumstances
Forced me to give it

I guess I needed humbling
That's why I went tumbling

Down a hill
Of decrease and release

How do I accomplish soaring?
My thirst to overcome is roaring

Rest assured,
I know a Mighty Captain

Who will navigate me
To a higher mountain.

Risen

Like Jesus rose,
So do I

Wipe your tears,
Turn up your frown

Nothing and no one
Can keep God's children down.

One in A Million

More precious than rubies,
I'm one of a kind

I'm Divine, fine,
A delectable red wine

The best thing about me?
I only get better with time-

My love and wisdom,
The depths of my mind

My quirks are mine,
Impossible to find-
In another, don't bother

I'm one in a hundred thousand times a dime.

Destiny Helpers

God, send me
To the places
With the people
Who recognize
My uncamouflaged essence

Those who will speak
Life into me
And bring clarity
Through their presence

Those who will testify
Of Your goodness
And speak of You
With passionate reverence

Send into my domain
The kind of support
That'll pulse through my veins
And make life sweeter than ever

I, too, desire to be a channel
Used to make their being
As light as a feather

Numerous great minds
Thinking alike

Iron sharpening iron
Making the other more precise

Gravitating into destiny
Escorted by
Unquestionable chemistry

We're unintended to travel alone.

Paradox

Both a realist
And an idealist

A paradox,
If you will

Needing the two
To keep balance
Both concepts revealed

Together, a tether
Bringing worlds apart
As one

Like when the moon vanishes
And a new day
Brings the sun.

Together

That burden of yours
Is no longer mine to carry

I filled in when I could,
But that load got too heavy

I can point you
To my Healer

And support you
Along the way

I can encourage your faith walk
And join you to pray

I can't hitch your traumas
When I'm spent
From mending my own

Let's learn
To support one another

As we both journey home.

An Ode to Music

Music is my advocate
Always helping
To regulate

The ebbs and flows
Of life

Music is a cleanser
For the acne
Of life's strife

Realigning my nervous system
From dysregulation,

Confirming personal experiences,
Debunking "I feel so alone" speculations

I just received
Miraculous relief
Through enchanting melodies

I just connected
With a stranger
Through lyrical testimonies

I just acquired inspiration

To get through
This new day

I just felt my soul groovin'
Telling me
“It’s gon' be okay"

Thank God for music;
The power that it has to heal

Glory for His creative formula
His will to be revealed

Through praise,
Beautiful sounds

And heaps
Of creative mounds

Called genres
Becoming mantras

I'm reignited,
Reunited,
Renewed.

Time Will Tell

Life, itself, is a test

I'm bubbling in
What I think
Is the right answer
And writing short responses

But no one told me
That every now and again,

These lines
Wouldn't be long enough

For the complexity
Of my thoughts

And that most times,
Wisdom cannot be bought

Some answers
can only be retrieved
As you live
And become stretched

Milestones of your journey,
You'll inevitably fetch

Time will tell.

Unveiled, Exhaled

I groaned
And I moaned

I struggled
Against my ego

I pleaded
And I begged

I swung at my fears

I ran out of options
Then let God's voice
Become clear

I stopped running
And trying to hide

I spoke gently
To my ego

And Became acquainted
With my pride

"I know
You want to keep me safe…

I know that you feel
The need to be in control

But know that you can no longer be master
Over the direction
Of my soul"

I let Love unveil me,
Now I can finally exhale, freely.

Love Is...

What the world tells us
About love is a lie.

Love is not blind
Love is patient,
Love is kind

Love can fly,
Love can defy
All odds and gravity
Love is an ally

Love can transmute
And filters out filth
True love squares up
To box burdensome guilt

Love ain't wishy washy
Always ready to up and leave

Love holds on
And unconditionally breathes...
Life into the crevices
Of your deepest,
Heaviest baggage

Love wants you to recover
As if that heartbreak
Never happened

Love is rooted
In unshakable Truths,
Love is the foundation
Of existence's roots

Love won't shame you
When you bellow out
In your deepest pain

Love will reassure you
That your crying out
Isn't in vain

Love will keep you
And willingly water your joy
Love won't play you
Like a cheap, temporary toy

Love is eternal
Love is unconditional
True Love is healthy
Because it's nutritional

I wanna be more like Love
In its purest form
I choose to rebel
I refuse to conform

I wanna let Love heal me
And empower me
To live at liberty

I wanna share Love's graces and mercies,
limitlessly.

www.ingramcontent.com/pod-product-compliance
Lightning Source LLC
Chambersburg PA
CBHW051746130826
49812CB00033B/1031
* 9 7 8 9 3 5 7 4 4 1 4 2 1 *